AGILE PROJECT MANAGEMENT

Quick-Start Guide For Beginners And How To Implement Agile Step-By-Step

Learn Agile Project Management Step-By-Step

TABLE OF CONTENT

INTRODUCTION

Agile project management usually refers to a group of software development methodologies largely based on iterative development as requirements and solutions move through self-organizing multi-functional teams. The term Agile Project Management was coined in 2001 when the Agile Manifesto was created.

Agile project management usually aims to promote constant change and inspection; it is centered on teamwork and leadership as well as solo work that develop both customer needs and company goals.

The concept behind Agile project management can be found in modern approaches to analysis and management such as Six Sigma, soft system methodology and speech act theory.

Agile project management methods are sometimes discussed as being the other end of the spectrum from so-called 'disciplined' or 'plan-driven' methods of working. This opinion is not strictly correct as it suggests that agile methods are not disciplined or planned. In reality, agile methods work on a continuing improvement level with constant adoption in order to keep up to date.

Agile systems are constantly being compared to adaptive systems which are changing to solve real problems and issues so that when the needs of a particular project begin to change the adaptive team will also change to fit too. The downside to adaptive systems is that they will have difficulty predicting what will happen in the future.

On the other hand, predictive methods tend to focus on planning the future in great detail. A predictive team can report exactly what features and tasks are planned for the entire length of the development process yet predictive teams have difficulty changing direction.

The main principles behind agile management systems are; priority of individual's actions over actions of tools and processes, customer collaboration over contact detail, the ability to respond to a challenge in a positive manner.

CHAPTER 1

WHAT IS AGILE PROJECT MANAGEMENT?

Agile project management generally describes a group of software development methods, which have been around for over ten years now and have continued to grow in popularity with all kinds of organizations, both large and small and by no means restricted to the software industry.

Working with Agile methodologies allows organizations to improve their product quality and also helps them to make sure those products and services can be brought to the market quickly and professionally.

When a company or organization begins to manage their projects using Agile project management methods, it is typical to see a marked increase in their growth and general expansion due to the high levels of productivity that are associated with Agile.

This project management method promotes and responds to change in an organic way, enabling a far more flexible approach to project development.

Whilst this approach is very different to more traditional methods whereby the outcome of the project is planned thoroughly and the outcome is fixed, that does not mean that Agile project management has an undisciplined approach to working on a project.

The end result with Agile project management is always a little less predictable, in comparison with old methods, but this is not necessarily a disadvantage.

Because this method adapts to change in a positive way, responding to issues as they arise and resolve them, the result is always far more successful than the results obtained by a team who are simply plowing forward blindly towards their end goal without ever seeming to consider a change of direction.

Agile project management encourages healthy and productive working relationships with colleagues who share accountability for the outcome of each project and work together to reach their goal.

Regular team meetings play a key role in the success of this teamwork and make sure that everyone is focused and working effectively.

At these vital meetings, the team can be brought up to date on the progress that has already been made, before making plans together about the next stage of the process and preparing for its completion.

Team members organize themselves without the need for a project manager and their shared skills mean they are able to carry out tasks effectively by assigning each task to the most suitable team member.

The ideal scenario when working on projects through Agile is for all parties working on the project to be housed under the same roof (i.e. one office) and in many ways, this gives workers the opportunity to forge stronger relationships and certainly offers more convenience.

But this is not crucial and it can be quite straightforward to apply the principles of Agile with success in a broad range of other situations thanks to the fantastic array of technology we have at our fingertips to aid communication with one another.

The present state of the economy means that competition is tough and there is a great deal of emphasis on performance. Agile project management brings a lot to the table.

Through its forward thinking approach that is centered on teamwork and collaboration, Agile project management helps organizations to compete and keep up with the pace in a fast-changing, diverse global market.

In terms of practicality and flexibility, Agile delivers far more effectively than any of the more traditional methods and is, therefore, a highly useful option to explore.

WHEN IS AGILE PROJECT MANAGEMENT NECESSARY?

If it's implemented correctly then agile project management can benefit every project manager out there to some degree. Agile project management is a less restrictive approach to project management. It caters for a far more interactive and flexible process.

Whilst this seems to initially go against the tradition of being organized, working to set timeframes and within set parameters, there are instances when it is essential. It is most often used in projects that require the development of software.

It is the most effective form of project management for any project that includes high levels of change and risk over a short period of time.

This approach does also bring a new set of challenges to the table. With flexibility comes an increased chance of things going awry.

In order to combat this, we must ensure the foundations of the team are built around honesty, excellent communication, and discipline.

These attributes correctly implemented will ensure the whole team stays focused and keeps moving in the correct direction, even through periods of change.

HOW TO BENEFIT?

The true key to success in project management is a balance. It means knowing not just the correct practices to implement, but also the correct importance and time that should be spent on each one.

There are aspects of agile project management that will impact any project in a positive manner.

The increased focus on team management and group accountability always leads to a happier more productive team. A happier team leads to a more productive team, which is never a bad thing.

The ability to adapt builds creativity and innovation at the ground level. This means problem-solving and potential obstacles are dealt with much more efficiently.

The increased interaction with customers allows the team to gain a better understanding and consistently deliver more reliable results.

Planning for the unknown is an essential ingredient of agile project management. Creating contingencies for problems can't be a bad thing.

1.   BUILD A TEAM TO SUIT YOUR APPROACH

When you are planning for a project with attributes suggesting agile project management is the best way to proceed, then building your team with the approach in mind can greatly increase the ease with which you work.

The ideal team will be energetic, innovative, and welcoming of change. Include all team members at every stage of planning, allowing you to ensure the deadlines can be met, and highlighting any potential problems that may need contingencies creating.

Once the project is underway ensuring you're in constant contact with all key team members.

Making yourself available will minimize the time needed to solve problems and answer questions, and maximize the effects of good communication and teamwork.

As you become more comfortable with agile projects, maybe by attending an agile project management training course, you will start to see the way in which it can be used to benefit most projects.

CHAPTER 2

HOW TO EXECUTE AGILE PROJECT MANAGEMENT?

The crux of all strategies is successful execution. Many managers are quick and proficient at planning, but unfortunately, fail when it comes down to implementing the strategy. Successful APM (Agile project management) is built upon two factors.

- Quick information flow

- Comprehending decisions right away

Agile project execution promotes decision sustaining information and gives team member the autonomy, which drives brilliance in execution. Agile project management is an advancement of successful management strategies.

It promotes communication, results, teamwork, and responsiveness making use of conventional tools of management. It offers a holistic approach to establishing strategy, plans, results, and employees.

You could do all this with Agile project management:

- Rehash management for the broader perspective

- Develop equality of information

- Enlarge the scale of employee autonomy

It has been observed that almost 90 percent of the devised strategies fail badly due to poor execution. As a matter of fact plans always fail when they lack confident, quick and attainable execution.

The failure of execution also originates due to various other factors, such as unclear accountability, lack of communication, vaguely defined duties and responsibilities, lack of focus and inadequate monitoring.

Furthermore, when plans fail due to poor execution, many employees get discouraged and as a result, the company incurs additional losses in the form of low productivity levels.

Today, a vast majority of business execution tactics are costly, complex and time-consuming. Six Sigma is an excellent example of conventional execution methods.

In fact, all the Agile methods promote teamwork, results, and collaboration. They process flexibility during the lifecycle of a project. The key is to adapt the plan to simplify the information flow in an organization. This will lead to right decisions at the right time.

TO EXECUTE AGILE PROJECT MANAGEMENT?

1.   Share

Sharing the vision and establishing clear goals will assist in aligning the organization with its strategic plan.

2.   Track

Numerical results are a major basis of decision support information.

3.   Analyze

The regular analysis gives quick access to many critical decision support data and facilitates the stakeholders in acting autonomously.

4.   Reevaluate

When supported by previous decision support data reevaluation, the goals of the business offer an effective change.

5.   Repeat

Goals, plans, and metrics might change but the systematic approach to successful execution must not.

HOW TO INTRODUCE AGILE PROJECT MANAGEMENT TO YOUR ORGANIZATION?

1.   Don't call it 'Agile': The word 'Agile' can come with bad connotations such as 'corner cutting' or 'passing fad', which makes companies skeptical about adopting the framework. Many of the agile practices, however, can be used in isolation to promote your cause.

Start to introduce concepts such as 'prioritized lists' and 'kanban visual boards', without calling them 'Agile techniques'. People will start to see the benefits and not even realize they're doing Agile.

2.   Death by Trial: People don't want to hear you endlessly evangelize the concept of Agile. You need to show success in order to get adoption. The best way to do this is to run a 2-week trial iteration.

Ask the business to give you their 100% trust for the entire duration of the iteration. In return for their trust, tell them that 'they win' if you can't deliver and they're not impressed.

3.   Phone a Friend: It's important to have allies when introducing new concepts to any environment. Find a champion within the business (Project Manager, Stakeholder) and show them how their life will be easier with Agile.

You could, for example, highlight to a project management that since the team is responsible for updating tasks themselves, there are less day-to-day management responsibilities.

You could also highlight to a key stakeholder that there's better risk management because the constant plan-implement-review nature of agile detects problems earlier.

4.   Make them feel they're not alone: To win over the business's support, you can show examples of industry leaders in this space.

5.   Listen to them! Ask the business about the challenges they're facing on their current projects. Provide an example of how Agile could potentially address each challenge.

The business will appreciate that you're listening to them and trying to solve their problems, rather than just evangelizing agile.

AGILE ADVANTAGES

With dynamically changing market scenarios dominating the outsourcing markets, it has become imperative to remain conversant with emergent technologies and use them for developing projects.

New platforms and technologies have a lot to offer in terms of reduced development time and targeting a wider range of client-centric requirements, however, while reaping the benefits they offer, they also impose a few constraints regarding their applicability.

Offshoring businesses can increase the productivity levels and generate higher profits but often face problems in finding technical teams familiar with the usage and implementation of new technologies.

For most organizations, it is more profitable to find technical talent in other countries and outsource their projects depending upon the nature and scope of the project on hand.

It is very important to manage projects in an effective manner to make them profitable. Several project management frameworks and methods aim to make project management easier and more effective.

Some of the popular methods used in the past, and even now are:

- Critical Path Method (CPM)

- Critical Chain Project Management (CCPM)

- PMI/PMBOK Method

- Event Chain Methodology (ECM)

- Extreme Project Management (XPM)

- Adaptive Project Framework (APF)

- Lean Development (LD)

- Six Sigma/Lean Six Sigma

- Dynamic Systems Development Model (DSDM)

- Feature Driven Development (FDD)

- Rapid Application Development (RAD)

- Systems Development Life Cycle (SDLC)

- Waterfall (Traditional)

Each method proposes to make project management easy and more accurate. Often, it is difficult to choose which method one ought to adopt for developing a project since every management technique has its own pros and cons.

While a particular organization may offer a positive feedback regarding a method it is following, consultants might consider it a bad choice and speak against it. There are no postulates or rules which define a "successful" project.

Also, there are no rules which can help in deciding whether a particular methodology is more effective as compared to the other. It is based more on personal experience, understanding how a methodology works and what it has to offer, and how well it can be implemented.

Perhaps, the most important aspect to understand is whatever methodology you choose, what is more, important is how well you use it to your benefit to make your project successful.

Projects may vary in terms of their scope, size, complexity, and nature. However, regardless of that, offshore or distributed teams have to be properly coordinated and managed.

Agile project management framework offers several options for managing remotely developed projects.

AGILE FRAMEWORKS

- Scrum

Recommended for developing small to medium sized projects using a team of 7 to 12 cross-functional and multi-skilled individuals. The Scrum framework is characterized by its clearly defined events, artifacts, roles, and process which have to be followed by the entire team.

The error correction and retrospection activities take precedence over documentation and delegation of authority. The client is actively involved in verifying the development carried out by the team.

The Scrum team delivers the business value in the project through successful product increments developed through periodic cycles known as sprints.

- Extreme Programming (XP)

Extreme Programming (XP) offers a practical approach to program development and focuses primarily on the delivery of business results.

It follows an incremental, start-with-something approach towards product development, and makes use of continued testing and revision processes.

XP is generally recommended for short-term projects, and development teams typically follow the code-test-analyze-design-integrate process.

XP is known for "paired" programming i.e. two developers engaged with code development and testing simultaneously. One programmer creates the code while other tests it on the spot.

- Kanban

Based upon the concept of Toyota production model, Kanban offers a pragmatic approach to development by matching the actual amount of work in progress to the development team's capacity in delivering it.

The framework provides more flexibility in terms of planning options, quicker output, a clear focus pertaining what needs to be developed, and maintaining total transparency throughout the product development cycle.

- Scaled Agile Frameworks (SAFe)

Scaled Agile Framework (SAFe) is a structured and prescriptive method to help large organizations and enterprises to get started with adopting Agile.

It is a popular and efficient Agile framework successfully used by many companies covering various industry verticals.

It is specially recommended for large sized software based projects where teams can function interdependently.

- Nexus

Nexus is an Agile framework focusing upon cross-team dependencies and team integration issues. It facilitates Agile implementation in complex and large-scale projects.

It functions as an exoskeleton and helps multiple Scrum teams to integrate and pursue a common goal of delivering valuable product increments through sprints.

Each team delivers a certain business value to the client through each product increment cycle, and the teams achieve this by following Agile principles and process.

Nexus is recommended for development teams consisting of over 100 individuals.

AGILE FOR DISTRIBUTED TEAMS

While executing your very first remote project, the most logical thing to do is to document the project vision and figure out how the team will deliver the project goals.

Proper and effective communication is of paramount importance while explaining the goals and objectives to team members.

It is a simple and straightforward process most of the times, but while working with distributed teams, the cultural differences and varying language proficiency levels may often create constraints and lead to miscommunication as well as confusion.

This can be a common scenario in case of teams located in countries across different time zones and possess limited ability to communicate using a particular language.

Individuals may find it difficult to understand and capture the exact project requirements and deliver code or functionality that does not fulfill end user requirements.

Projects often fail because of these and other such technical and non-technical reasons.

Using Agile it may be possible to simplify these types of problems. Agile is not a silver bullet that can rectify all issues and problems faced during project execution.

Agile is a framework, therefore It depends upon how well the team understands its principles and how effectively it implements them in the project.

However, the framework is designed such that issues can be dealt with in a more proactive and effectual manner.

DEALING WITH ISSUES USING AGILE

Businesses opt for remote or distributed teams mainly to segregate the development activity from the main organization body by translocating the team and development activity to some other location for management or financial reasons.

The team is directly employed by the organization and each member is an employee. In the case of offshoring, the entire project is outsourced to a development vendor who executes the project on behalf of the client or develops it as a part of the client contract.

This discussion does not try to differentiate between whether the remote team is a part of the parent organization or it belongs to an outsourcing vendor.

Some common issues faced while working with both types of teams are discussed and how those issues can be properly targeted using Agile. It is worthwhile to know that Agile is not the only project management platform to develop IT or software projects.

Neither does it offer a guaranteed way of dealing with issues faced while working with or employing remote teams. However, the framework is uniquely designed, and is flexible enough, to deal with such issues in a more effective manner, and more easily.

PROJECT VISION AND DOCUMENTATION

The project vision explains the goals and project deliverables. The primary aim of the team should be to deliver work supporting the vision so meaningful business value can be delivered to the client.

Often, development teams put in efforts and deliver work, but when reviewed by the client, it is discovered that the features developed don't exactly support what the client actually wants.

This can be a very common scenario when teams are unclear about what the project aims to achieve and why it exists in the first place. A common reason why teams may fail to understand the vision could be language barriers (In the case of distributed teams located in different countries and speaking different languages) or a lack of proper communication from the client's or management's side explaining the objectives.

Agile does not emphasize upon extensive documentation. In real life scenarios elaborate or extensive documentation often remains locked away in filing cabinets or resides on shelves for future references - teams rarely bother to read them thoroughly since they can be large in size and a lot of time is spent in reading and understanding them.

The attitude of most development teams (Don't mean to disrespect them in any way) is to get started with work so deadlines can be met. Teams are generally pressed for time so they don't bother, or can't afford to spend hours reading the comprehensive documentation.

Paperwork is greatly reduced in Agile, and if you choose to follow Agile, you need to create just enough documentation to get started with work. More importance is given to understanding client-centric requirements and delivering business value, rather than creating elaborate reports and documents.

Moreover, one of the responsibilities of the product owner in Agile is to ensure that the team understands the deliverables and project vision properly before it starts to work.

The PO also makes sure that the business value delivered from the sprints is useful and matches the project vision.

MAINTAINING QUALITY STANDARDS

Quality and deadlines are two most important factors associated with, and affecting, the success levels of a project.

Quality features fulfilling end user requirements have to be developed within the decided time so it can be properly marketed and business returns availed from it.

In the IT market segment it is not just important to build quality software, but to release it in the correct manner at the correct time and at the correct place (targeted market audience i.e. the geographical boundaries within which end users are likely to buy your product.

With online marketing these boundaries remain virtual but nevertheless play an important part in deciding the "target audience" when the project is planned and incepted).

When outsourcing work to remote teams, the quality aspects could get compromised upon if a QA or testing process in setting up as a part of development process. Fewer development teams actually bother to test the code for regression after it is developed unless it is a pre-decided activity and integrated with the development process.

The Agile manifesto states "Our highest priority is to satisfy the customer through the early and continuous delivery of valuable software."

Its emphasis on "early and continuous delivery of valuable software" i.e. useful and valuable product features should be developed and delivered to the client on regular basis.

Agile focuses on the delivery of "shippable" features. Each feature should be properly tested for errors and made bug free before its development can be considered as complete and deployable. Developers and programmers often double as testers to carry out the QA part during sprint cycles.

Agile fails if "workable" features are not developed. Remote teams trained in Agile have to fulfill the test conditions stated in the acceptance criteria defined for each development task created in the product backlog (ideally).

THE SUPERVISOR OR PROJECT MANAGER'S ROLE

Every project needs a manager to oversee its execution and completion. It is important for the supervisor or the project manager to remain available to the team and resolve problems and issues as and when they occur.

When teams are located on-premises it becomes easy to resolve technical problems since face-to-face interactions are possible and the manager is always available when you need him or her.

That is not always the case with remote or distributed teams. Owing to time differences, the manager could be ending the day while the remote team would be just about to start with work.

Teams may be required to wait for some time before problems are resolved, and this could delay work further. Deadlines and commitments may therefore not be met.

The Scrum Master's role is very clearly defined in the Agile framework. The SM often plays a servant-leader role, and mentors and facilitates the Agile process. The SM ensures that he or she is always available to the team and resolves glitches whenever the team gets stuck.

In Agile, the Scrum Master is a specific role played by a person, rather than a designation or responsibilities given to a single individual. The role can be played by anyone in the team. In the case of distributed teams, a responsible team member can be taught to play the Proxy Scrum Master's role and provided with quick-access channels to communicate with the actual SM or PO in the case of urgent issues.

The person also functions as a team representative and creates daily feedback reports which can be studied by the client, PO, and the SM as per their convenience.

OWNERSHIP AND TEAM EMPOWERMENT

Traditional project management methods differentiate between senior and junior level individuals, and have a clear hierarchical structure defining authority levels and who reports to whom.

Even today, most organizations still follow this traditional hierarchical model, and individuals belonging to different levels of authority remain concerned about their responsibilities and reporting status.

Even though the model is organized, it takes a lot of time for issues to get resolved as the escalation process involves several individuals starting from the junior level to senior levels.

Moreover, people have a tendency to "pass on" issues to senior levels personnel and let them decide what to do next. Technical staff and junior level employees may prefer not to get involved with decision making since they often become scapegoats to bureaucratic procedures.

In the case of distributed teams, the scenario can become even worse because you don't have to deal with just bureaucratic attitudes but the language and distance factor may further make the team even less accountable for the success or failure of the project.

Agile does not believe in shifting responsibilities or escalating issues. As per the model, teams are cross-functional and self-managing. Each team member often takes up additional tasks other than his or her particular skillet thereby reducing the total numbers of skilled members required in the team.

There are no senior-subordinate levels - just three primary roles of the product owner, scrum master, and the development team. Rather than assigning tasks, each team member voluntarily takes up work based upon his or experience and skills.

One of the most important aspects about Agile is that the team has to "own" the project on behalf of the client. It means each person is responsible not just for the work done by him or her, but the overall contribution of all members at the team level is even more important.

The entire team is accountable for the success or failure of the project - not just the product owner but each and every member of the team.

CHAPTER 3

AGILE PROJECT MANAGEMENT VS TRADITIONAL PROJECT MANAGEMENT

Tipped to be the hottest trend in project management, Agile has seen its heyday come at last. Not a new concept, agile project management has been used to some degree in the software industry for several decades, but is only now coming to the fore as a workable project management method for other industries too.

Using agile project management techniques is not a million miles away from traditional methods.

You still do the same work and arrive at the same end goal, but with the agile method work tends to be faster, more productive and risks tend to be diminished. Here's why.

TRADITIONAL PROJECT MANAGEMENT

This method, also known as the waterfall method, is the most widely used form of project management worldwide. It typically involves six key steps from start to finish:

1.   Requirements

2.   Design

3.   Development

4.   Integration

5.   Testing

6.   Deployment

Each one stage is completed before the whole team moves onto the next stage, making this sequential method seem like something of a waterfall cascade, hence the name.

Not all projects include all stages, and some may include a few more, but in essence, this is the formation of waterfall project management.

Traditional PM is widely accepted as being valuable for smaller, well-designed projects, but can sometimes struggle when dealing with larger and less well-defined situations.

It is designed for use in construction and manufacturing industries, where later changes are impossible or not cost effective, meaning everything needs to be done in a certain order.

AGILE PROJECT MANAGEMENT

The agile method differs in that everything can take place in any order, and is not necessarily sequentially completed. The method relies on human interaction management and works on the project as a set of small tasks which are defined and completed as the demand arises.

Large projects can be simply broken down into smaller components, known as 'sprints', and tackled for a short space of time until complete.

In agile, the design, testing, integration, and development are all undertaken during each sprint, which makes the likelihood of errors being built into the final project much less.

This means there may be major changes made throughout the lifespan of the project, and the final product might not be exactly what was envisaged at the start. It will, if done right, be relevant, useful and flawless.

AGILE PROJECT MANAGEMENT AGAINST TRADITIONAL MANAGEMENT MODELS WHICH IS BEST?

The most suitable method for managing your project is something you will need to decide for yourself. It will largely depend on the type of project you are delivering, as well as the scale.

Projects involving creative industries or software development benefit much more naturally from agile than those involved in creating physical products, as they allow for changes to be made even at very late stages in the project delivery.

Consider how stable the requirements of the project are. Projects that are likely to undergo changes to the brief or the requirements will respond much better to an agile project management framework, whereas those with well-defined business requirements and where certain stages need to be completed before moving on are more suited to traditional project management.

AGILE IMPLEMENTATION MAKING PROJECT MANAGEMENT -BECOME AGILE

Agile methodologies were originally developed in an effort to enhance the process of software development through an approach aimed at minimizing the time, resources and incidence of error in the final product.

Traditionally, even slight changes in project requirements could upset the whole development cycle and it would be difficult to predict the quality of outcome and the time spent on fixing any possible errors.

However, agile processes helped to reduce the development life cycle into manageable delivery cycles in which the software product could be developed in functional segments and tested for any possible flaws to ensure that they are working as required.

HOW CAN AGILE METHODOLOGIES BE OF HELP?

This approach allowed the Developers to assimilate almost any big or small changes at any stage of the project without affecting the quality of the end product. In this way, product functionalities could be tested, reviewed and improved upon much in advance of delivering the end product in its entirety.

This led to major cost reductions and lesser time was spent on taking corrective measures in the final stages of the project with overall improved efficiency resulting in a win-win situation.

Project Managers were quick to realize that agile methodologies could have industry-wide applications and by adopting agile processes non-IT project management could also be made that much more efficient and cost-effective.

Some of the steps integral to making a project agile are:

Scan

At the first sign of change, agile development relies on keeping an eye out for emerging trends and patterns which can help understand new conditions better.

Analyze

Take into account any new information and knowledge available and chalk out plans accordingly. This would help keep pace with changing conditions and not be left behind in work goals.

Respond

After identifying areas that present potential risks and opportunities, develop responsive strategies to take advantage of opportunities and mitigate risks.

Change

Transforming existing policies and processes with a view to make them more inclusive in terms of ongoing changes and enhance the overall adaptability of the workflow as a result.

Traditional Sequential Project Management, also known as Waterfall Project Management is best suited for projects where the level of uncertainty is comparatively low and requirements are not supposed to change much in the duration of the project.

On the other hand, Agile Project Management thrives on assimilating change and exploring diverse solutions to make the project development more flexible and overcome unforeseen hurdles at any stage of development process.

HOW AGILE PROJECT DEVELOPMENT WORKS?

Efficient collaboration and communication hold the key to setting agile development in motion by bringing everyone on board and helping understand the approach embodied in agile processes.

The project development is broken up into various segments and tasks are sub-divided and smaller time segments are assigned for completing each of these tasks.

This is known as incremental project development, allowing for review at every stage of development instead of waiting for project completion.

After every stage of the project, the design and functionality of completed project tasks can be evaluated against current requirements and suitable improvements can be made.

The tasks can then be re-evaluated at regular intervals and in this way, improvement, innovation, and diversification in terms of solutions become the basis for development of an ongoing project.

This leads to efficient utilization of available time and resources and creates greater space for experimentation and exploring alternatives wherever traditional approaches to planning do not yield satisfactory results.

These are also the reasons why agile development is so much in demand these days.

Whether it is software development, a construction project or a project leading to the creation of any specific product or service, agile processes help enhance the productivity while working within the time and scope of the project.

Through adoption of agile methodologies, an organization can not only make its processes more efficient but also improve its organizational culture as a whole.

CHAPTER 4: AGILE PROJECT MANAGEMENT THE WAY TO GO IN AN ORGANIZATION?

Constant innovation and development, both are required to make things work in any organization. Over time the procedures and work methodologies followed by development team changes.

Instead of deploying traditional methods or 'waterfall' techniques they are switching to agile methodology. The problems with traditional technology are plenty; the major one is of 'freezing the requirements' after blueprint is designed. This makes it difficult and expensive to alter anything after most of the work on a project is done.

WHY IS AGILE PROJECT MANAGEMENT DEEMED AS THE BEST?

1.   Clients can track changes

Gone are the days when clients were least interested in the development process developers follow. Today time equals money, where they want to get things done in the best possible way and as quickly as possible. This technology provides them with a definite set of benefits where they can keep full control over the entire process.

He can set a proper timeframe within which the project needs to be delivered. He is allowed to make changes in the requirements and priorities anytime if he wishes to do so. This increases customer's satisfaction.

2.   Gives fast return on investments

Agile is the best trick to achieve faster returns on investments. This methodology is not just helpful for working for clients, but also for your own products.

You can develop a product across iterations and can keep adding more features to it. This can give an extra edge to an organization, where they can launch a product with limited features and keep on adding the premium features afterward.

3.   Keeps the risk levels low

Regular feedback from prospective clients is a great way to reduce market risk. Getting a timely feedback from prospect clients can assist in making the product better and reduce the risk of not meeting their expectations.

The project is easily accessible to the clients during its life cycle. Even if the client wants to make a cancellation in the early stages, you can easily handle that. Thus, it imparts better accessibility and visibility to clients in order to make correct decisions.

4.   Better management process

Agile methodology leverages certain benefits to the management team in an organization. As the entire developmental process is pretty much predictable, there is a good chance for better workforce management. The relationship between clients and team members also gets better, which create better future prospects.

5.   Enhanced product quality

Agile methodologies generally result in best quality products. When the experts and clients are in constant contact, clients can always ask experts about the best possible technology that can be followed.

Cross-functional development teams including developers, testers, programmers, analysts, and writers work together as a single team. Their collaborative efforts will automatically result in the best quality and reliable product.

Agile methodology offers a new and extremely productive way of handling projects. It leverages enhanced quality and lowers risk levels. It does break all the rules of traditional development without compromising on speed and reliability.

The best part of the agile methodology is that it keeps everyone working on the project happy be it client or organization.

CONSIDER AGILE SOFTWARE COMPANY FOR YOUR IT NEEDS

The agile software company has increased and raised in the market today. It has brought about more focus on the agile software development, where methods on developments of software are grouped and based on the iterative and incremental developments.

It is of great importance since with the use of this software, it has enhanced and promoted adaptive planning.

They are with the aim of how to make more investments, attracting more customers on the use of adopting agile software, to improve delivery effectiveness.

The company also has brought about evolutionary development and delivery effectiveness, which is timed as interactive approach and encourages rapid and flexible response to change.

They develop product chain management solutions, with the use of agile software, hence enabling manufacturers and partners involved in the business to build on better, more profitable products in a faster and more efficient way.

It has a manifesto that tends guide the entire organization, in providing and inventing better ways of developing the software. By doing this, the companies are able to involve in strategic ways of developing the software in various ways, such as by providing training to the agile customers and other companies on the usefulness of the software.

Coaching is another method, used by many other agile software companies, to pass on the information, or rather the advantageous of using agile as an IT resource. The agile industry is able to offer consultancy on a mode of helping other software companies, as well as consumers, to support agile and hence adopt the changes, brought about by the software to the IT market today.

There are steps involved in the process of developing software, which is considered by the company to be ways of building and modifying the software more.

The agile methods include agile modeling, agile unified process which is AUP, dynamic system development method, essential unified process, extreme programming, feature driven development, open unified process, scrum and velocity tracking.

These methods are rather the most used and preferred, this is because the processes involved are quite efficient for the advancement of the agile software.

The agile software has a development life cycle support of how it came to be in existence; this is best explained by the use of agile methods, which tend to focus on different aspects to bring about the software. With the use of this cycle, agile has brought about the solutions that tend to drive the product innovation, and introduction process.

The focus has been kept by the agile software company on the practices such as extreme programming, pragmatic programming, agile modeling among others; the company has also focused on the managing software's projects or rather the scrum.

Among the methods used to develop agile, there are approaches that tend to give full coverage on the advancement, while others are suited for requirements to a specified phase of the development life cycle of the software.

The measure of quantifying agile software has been an issue, hence many approaches have been brought forward so as to measure its quantity.

The practical application of quantifying agile has not yet been seen, but with the proposed agility measuring index, the score projects have been achieved by a number of factors such as duration, the risk involved, novelty, effort and as well as interaction.

With the use of this and other techniques involved, the agile software company has based all this on measurable goals, as well as by the use of agile self-assessments to determine if another group uses agile practices.

CHAPTER 5

SCRUM AND AGILE PRINCIPLE

Many software development companies are striving to become more Agile and the Scrum is the agile buzzword at the moment.

The problem is that some companies or teams want to adopt Scrum just because they read about it on the internet and they are sure that if it is a simple agile framework it must be very easy using it. Besides, who wouldn't want to be more agile in these days?

Some people start using Scrum although they know almost nothing about the Scrum. Yes, all they know about Scrum is that you have to work in some iterations called "Sprint".

And at the end of the project, they are so disappointed because the project was not as successful as they expected. That is because the Scrum is dramatically different from traditional sequential development.

Every Scrum team member must be familiar with the basic principle of Scrum.

Here is the first principle:

- Our highest priority is to satisfy the customer through the early and continuous delivery of valuable software.

- At the start of the new project you have to answer the one really big question, what exactly are we building? The short answer is that you must build the software that is going to be of value to the customer and will satisfy their needs. But in the reality, it is not so simple to achieve that.

In the sequential development project, you would first start with a lengthy up-front requirement-gathering phase.

The result of this phase would be hundreds of pages of detailed requirements documentation where all features are equally important. Let's face it, the customer doesn't care about documents and UML diagrams and it is hard to get the right information from the customer and put it on the paper.

They just want to get the software that maximizes the added value to their business and they don't know exactly what that value is on the first day of the project.

There is a big chance that there will be some disappointment on the customer side when the software will be presented for the first time at the end of the project, although the software works as at it is described it the documentation.

There is a totally different story with Scrum teams which adapt the early and continuous delivery of valuable software because the client is involved throughout the lifetime of the project.

That is how you can get early customer feedback and valuable emergent requirements. Scrum team documents all the features in a product backlog, which is a master list of all desired functionality not yet in the product. The product backlog is also known as prioritized feature list and priority is assigned based on the items of most value to the business or that offer the earliest ROI and value.

Product owner has to groom the product backlog continuously because items are added, removed and reprioritized each sprint as more is learned about the product being developed.

The result is that the most important and highest-priority items are implemented first because they are found at the top of the product backlog.

PRINCIPLES OF PROJECT MANAGEMENT

The key principles based upon the project management framework, designed to improve the likelihood of your project succeeding.

1.   Business justification: Every project should lead to a worthwhile return on investment. In other words, we need to understand the benefits that a particular project will bring, before committing ourselves to any significant expenditure.

During the lifecycle of a project, however, circumstances can change quickly. If at any point it becomes clear that a return on investment is no longer feasible, then the project should be scrapped and no more money wasted.

2.   Defined roles and responsibilities: Everybody working on the project needs to understand the nature of their involvement: for what is each person responsible, and to whom are they accountable? Without clear roles and responsibilities, nobody will know precisely what he or she is supposed to be doing (and everybody will pass the buck at the first sign of trouble).

In such a chaotic environment, the progress of the project will be seriously jeopardized.

3.   Manage by exception: Project sponsors should avoid getting too bogged down in the day-to-day running of projects and instead allow the project manager to concentrate on this area.

Micro-management by a sponsor is a hindrance, not a help.

Project sponsors should set clear boundaries for cost and time, with which the manager should work.

If he/she cannot provide the agreed deliverables within these constraints, concerns must be escalated to the sponsor for a decision.

4.   Manage by stages: Break the project up into smaller chunks, or stages. Each stage marks a point at which the project sponsor will make key decisions.

For example, is the project still worthwhile? Are the risks still acceptable? Dividing a project into stages, and only committing to one stage at a time, is a low-risk approach that enables the sponsor to manage by exception.

5.   Focus on products: It is vital that clients and customers think carefully about the products or deliverables, they require before the project begins.

The clearer they can be about their requirements, the more realistic and achievable the plans that can be produced. This makes managing the project much easier and less risky.

6.   Learn from experience: don't risk making the same mistakes on every project; consider why certain aspects went well or badly, then incorporate the lessons learned into your approach to your next project.

Humans have an amazing capacity to learn, but when it comes to repeating errors made during previous projects, we all too often fail to learn the lessons.

7.   Tailor to suit the environment: Whatever project management methodology or framework you favor, it must be tailored to suit the needs of your project.

Rather than blindly following a methodology, the project manager must be able to adapt procedures to meet the demands of the work in hand. How you plan on a two-week project is likely to be very different from how you plan on a two-year project

This project management principle discussed can be applied universally, irrespective of language, geography or culture.

These principles have been proven in practice over many years; adhere to them, rather than struggle on without a coherent strategy, and you will have a greater chance of project success.

CHAPTER 6

AGILE SOFTWARE DEVELOPMENT TECHNIQUES

Handling your software projects with the fastest turnaround time possible requires agile software development. This is the most advanced form of software process involved.

The need of the hour is to employ innovative methods of creation of programming tools.

Attain greater productivity and improve quality in the flow of work. Product management is involved in the analysis, design and development, testing and implementation of the project.

There is a need for open collaboration which provides scope for open communication. Clients must be updated about the project on a timely basis in order to figure out defects in the initial stage itself. This allows for fixing of technical problems in its conceptualization stage itself.

With Agile software development, there is enough scope for change in project specification even in the last stage.

Arranging conference calls, sending weekly reports on the status of the project, project tracking and updating plans, implementation of innovative marketing strategies involve a good insight of the modern project management techniques.

Conduct meetings to supervise the product at every stage of development. Keep your communication channels open and incorporate the changes asked for. Do away with the flaws in the initial stage itself.

IMPORTANT STAGES OF THE PROJECT DEVELOPMENT

- Manufacturing a product

- Positioning it

- Branding

- Close observation on how it functions

- Modification

Before merchandising your software tool, you must understand your competitors. Compare their product with your features and update them before launching them in the market.

Conceptualization of your project launch is vital to the success of your launch. Figure out where your market lies and venture into it. Attain competitive information and gain an edge over the others.

USING AGILE SOFTWARE DEVELOPMENT TECHNIQUES FOR YOUR SUCCESS

Several methodologies began to rise in the late 90's and thus stimulated public attention particularly to software developers. Various combinations were formulated from old ideas, new ideas, and transmuted old ideas on every each methodology. Prior to that, they all emphasized close collaboration between the programmer team and business experts; face-to-face communication (as more efficient than written documentation);

frequent delivery of new deployable business value; tight, self-organizing teams; and ways to craft the code and the team such that the inevitable requ

irements mix-ups were not being led into crisis. In elaborative relation from those details mentioned, Agile Software Development uncovers better ways of developing software by doing it and helping others do it. Such principles or values are being extracted out from it as follows:

- Individuals and interactions over processes and agile tools

- Working software over comprehensive documentation

- Customer collaboration over contract negotiation

Subsequently to the formulation of the Agile Manifesto. The group of software development methodologies based on iterative development, where requirements and solutions evolve through collaboration between self-organizing and cross-functional teams.

The said Agile development generally promotes disciplined project management process that upholds such as:

- Frequent inspection and adaptation

- Leadership philosophy that encourages teamwork

- Self-organization and accountability

- Set of engineering best practices; of which allows rapid delivery of high-quality software

- Aligns development with customer needs and company goals as a business approach

As lots of studies and research are being carried out just for the betterment of the world of technology and information, agile development methods have grown technically by numbers of them.

Henceforth, they promote mostly with development iterations, teamwork, collaboration, and process adaptability throughout the life-cycle of the project.

The said methods are very efficient and organized wherein they break tasks into small increments with minimal planning, and do not directly involve long-term planning. Iterations are short time frames, such as the "time boxes", that typically last from one to four weeks.

Each iteration involves a team working through a full software development cycle including planning, requirements analysis, design, coding, unit testing, and acceptance testing when a working product is demonstrated to stakeholders.

Thus, it utterly helps minimize overall risk and lets the project adapt to changes quickly. Stakeholders produce documentation as required. Its goal is to have an available release after on every each iteration since multiples of them (products or new features) are expected to be released afterward, regarding the fact that a single iteration may not add enough functionality to warrant a guaranteed market release.

In relation about the collaboration between cross-functional and self-organizing team mentioned a while ago; a team composition in an agile project is usually of those that were mentioned, without consideration for any existing corporate hierarchy or the corporate roles of team members. Team members normally take responsibility for tasks that deliver the functionality an iteration requires.

They decide individually how to meet an iteration's requirements.

The methods thereof emphasize face-to-face communication over written documents when the team is all in the same location.

When a team works in different locations, they maintain daily contact through videoconferencing, voice, e-mail, etc.

Agile tools are being created in order to help development teams in their infinite search of the right and sufficient essential tools for software development.

The agile tools are as follows:

1.   JIRA Studio as a hosted development suite

Brings together Atlassian's products to give you agile project management, issue tracking, wiki collaboration, source code analysis and reviews, plus subversion to improve release planning, team communication, and customer feedback gathering.

Useful for: Developer, team lead, and product manager

Designed for: Planning, Lightning feedback and gathering customer feedback

2.   JIRA + Green Hopper for agile project management

Coupled with the Green Hopper plug-in, JIRA is the foundation of a powerful agile platform for developers to plan releases, gather feedback, track issues and manage project status.

Useful for: Developer, Team Lead, and Product Manager

Designed for: agile planning, gathering customer feedback and monitoring team performance

3.   Confluence for agile collaboration

Designed to help agile developers plan requirements, collaborate on changes and display metrics.

Useful for: Developers (internal blogging with peers), technical writers (develop docs) and product managers (collaborate on requirements and Balsamiq mockups)

Designed for: planning (PRDs and JIRA issues macro), lightning feedback (documenting changes, RSS + Dashboards) and team performance metrics (JIRA Issues macro + Bamboo builds plug-in)

4.   Fisheye for code analysis

With Fisheye's insight into a source code repository, agile developers can find code fast, get notified about relevant code changes and receive useful metrics on team performance.

Useful for: Developers (find code fast), Team Leads (metrics on the team and each developer) and Technical Leads (RSS for a branch)

Designed for: lightning feedback and team performance metrics

5.   Bamboo for continuous integration

Agile developers use continuous integration to get the most from their unit tests. Set up Bamboo to get instantaneous feedback on the impact of each commit and monitor build metrics.

Useful for: Developers (learn about their commits), Team Leads (get build stats fast) and Testers (perform integration and performance tests early in the game)

Designed for: Testing early and often (CI Whitepaper), lightning feedback (two- way IM) and team performance metrics

6.   Clover for code coverage

The ultimate Java code coverage tool for agile development, Clover accurately assesses the impact on your tests and notifies you of test coverage gaps before it is too late.

Useful for: Developers and testers

Designed for: Testing early and often and lightning feedback

7.   Crucible for code reviews

Integrates peer code review directly into your work habits. Agile developers use Crucible get timely feedback on their code and maintain metrics and an audit trail.

Useful for: Developer (Distributed review), Team lead (get developers to learn from each other) and Technical Lead (Get metrics on audit trail on who did what and why)

Designed for: Testing Early and often (pre-commit reviews), lightning Feedback (review notifications), Performance Metrics (reports and audit trail)

8.   Pyxis - creators of Green Hopper

Given by the certified trainers and by practitioners with industry expertise, Pyxis' training program provides effective techniques through practical exercises and group discussions to increase your knowledge of Agility and help your software development team build the right software.

Useful for: Developers, Team Leaders, Scrum Masters, Product Managers, and Product Owners

Designed for: Mastering Agile software engineering practices and developing innovative project management practices

The Agile tools given are some of the few tools that are being offered from Agile Software Development developers provided by the internet. Some tools vary accordingly from depending on its uses which are said to be well-tested.

CHAPTER 7

PROBLEMS IMPLEMENTING AGILE

Agile is an excellent development methodology, responsive to business changes with quick turnaround and highly visible results. The concept is in widespread use, particularly in software development, but having implemented Agile almost from the inception of Extreme Programming.

We've seen issues arise related to people being on Agile teams for extended periods of time. These can be mitigated or even avoided entirely if you know what to look for.

1.   Burnout is the most prevalent symptom of Agile: The pace of an Agile project is unrelenting. Unlike Waterfall and associated development methodologies, there are very few built-in times for team members to catch their collective breath and celebrate milestones.

To help combat burnout, try a few of these techniques:

- Set your own team goals, publicize them, and celebrate when you achieve them

- Move people among teams whenever possible to change the scenery, so to speak

- Report and celebrate small victories

- Set a periodic 'down' iteration/sprint where everyone can work on something they'd like to do (or rotate that ability amongst the team members). You'll get some interesting research, something to look forward to for the team members, and a break while still working.

2.   Meandering happens when people start on tasks/user stories but don't finish them. They might even agree to the goals for the day and end up working on some interesting bug that was far down the priority list. Sometimes this is related to burnout, sometimes you see it when the project manager or Scrum Master is away for a while, and sometimes people just are bored and distracted.

The best solution is to have a hard and fast rule about taking on more than a certain number of user stories (usually 1, not more than 2) unless one of the assigned stories has been officially been blocked. To enforce the rule, the project manager/Scrum Master will have to unassigned the offending user stories (past the limit) as soon as they're picked up to get people back on track.

3.   Stagnation materializes when people get so caught up in the short burst nature of the sprint user stories that they don't improve their skills or acquire new ones (hard skills and/or soft skills). Watch for stagnation carefully, since it can be a little hard to spot. Periodically assign user stories that stretch a team member's skills, even if there's someone else on the team who already has the skills.

Create some 'administrative' user stories to send people off to pick up a new skill that might be needed in upcoming user stories (people like to use their new skills and your project might get a nice shot in the arm). Finally, periodically ask in wrap-up meetings or daily meetings what new technologies, techniques, or processes the team members think might have a place in the project or be worth a try/evaluation.

The daily stand-up turns into a grind. This may take a little more work on the part of the project manager/Scrum Master. First, be sure you're keeping the meeting to the shortest time possible - it's stand-up for a reason. If it's over 15 minutes something is wrong.

The agenda is quite fixed - what did you finish, what do you plan, what are your blockers, so don't veer off the agenda (set separate meetings if needed so it doesn't get confusing). If two people need to discuss a strategy or a blocker, send them off to do it after the meeting (don't use the whole team's time). If someone runs too long every day talk to them in private and get them to make their part shorter.

You may want to schedule something just a little longer once a week if you have a team that wants to deal with process issues, etc., more often than once an iteration, but get the stand-up part of the meeting done first to avoid any confusion about the format.

Most importantly, make the meeting fun whenever you can. Bring something to eat, start with a joke, and pass around little awards.

You might encounter a secret move back to waterfall. When this happens, everyone keeps working within the general agile structure and the team often doesn't realize what's going on.

Symptoms include user stories that drag from sprint to sprint, user stories that are too big or broken down inappropriately, lack of or improper use of epics, and QA/Test organizations falling behind because they are handed too much functionality all at once. Don't let the team con you into waiting 'until the next big function' because it's 'too much trouble/delay/work' to fix the problem immediately.

CHAPTER 8

POINTERS TO HELP YOU KNOW IF YOU ARE "AGILE" OR NOT

It would be wonderful to know more about these versions, but a basic question always keeps on popping up - Is the client really following Agile in a true sense? Are you a hard-core Agile supporter or a ScrumBut? Maybe, it would be more worthwhile to ascertain whether you or your client, are in fact following Agile in the first place, let alone other scaled versions of Agile.

HERE ARE A COUPLE OF POINTERS TO HELP YOU KNOW IF YOU ARE "AGILE" OR NOT.

1.   Is development carried out through iterations?

Needless to say, the main purpose of implementing an Agile framework is to benefit through product increments in a consistent manner. Nobody can claim they're following Agile if their project development process does not support regular product increments at the end of sprints.

In addition to iterative development, the Agile implementation should also support dynamic collaboration - sharing of feedback and information amongst the product owner, scrum master, scrum team, and the stakeholders. Iterative development and collaborative nature are Agile trademarks, and it is most essential for organizations to support these features if they claim to be Agile.

2.   Can changes be incorporated during the product development cycle?

One of the main reasons why people opt for Agile is its ability to incorporate changes in the product definition even while the product development process is currently underway.

It is a unique selling feature of all Agile frameworks and is synonymous with developing a project while still maintaining its business value - at all times. Irrespective of the changes taking place in the market - whether big or small - the project development process should have, and retain, its capability to dynamically change the functionality developed, and offered, by the product features as and when necessary. Agile projects should support this feature.

3.   Can development be carried out in "bits and pieces" rather than "as a whole"?

Perhaps what makes Agile frameworks so unique are their iterative structures supporting daily sprints? In Scrum or XP, the product development is carried out in the form of daily sprints. Special events are held to plan the sprint (the sprint planning meeting) and ensure that proper and acceptable product increments are availed at the end of sprints (sprint reviews and retrospectives).

The development carried out in "bits and pieces" should result into shippable functionality (successfully developed user stories), and should also be acceptable to the project owners (stakeholders). "Small sized" consistent development, which is bug-free, should have the capability to later integrate in a correct functional manner so as to form the "complete" product - a euphemism which conveys "Development in pieces to be later integrated to form the actual product."

As on today, organizations are not just limited to using traditional versions of Agile frameworks. There are subtle variants, which can be scaled up or down as per the need, and which can be "tailored" to meet the unique project development needs of business concerns.

It may not be possible to state or define the exact set of parameters which a project management methodology, or framework, should satisfy to be considered Agile since Agile is all about "inspecting" and "adapting".

The main essence of Agile lies in its ability to change itself, it's working, and mold itself to suit the specific development related needs, as the case may be.

CHAPTER 9

AGILE MANIFESTO AND PRINCIPLES

Every business has a potential to grow and expand via agile development practices. Agile practices allow software developers to divide a large project into several modules.

Developers tackle each module at a time while making sure that it is completed within a preset period. After the completion of each module, the software owner is requested to verify if the completed software module is used.

Agile practices are preferred to traditional software development methods that require an in-house team of developers to do one project until it is over.

These traditional approaches do not involve the project owner until the work is finished. They, therefore, allow costly mistakes to be committed. Due to the unreliability of these methods, big and small organizations are turning to Agile developers for help.

Today numerous businesses meet their software creation goals via agile development practices. Projects that demand extra speed or technological expertise are generally assigned to nearshore or offshore agile developing teams.

These teams are preferred to in-house developers when an urgent project has to be performed creatively and accurately.

These teams are remote companies that do not involve a customer in person. They use latest methods of internet communication to get in touch with their customer until a software development project ends.

These communication methods include Skype, instant messengers and email chatting and messaging. Effective communication remains a vital component of agile development practices.

It unites development teams and consumers irrespective of the big distance between them. Agile practices are based on the stipulations of the Agile Manifesto.

This manifesto was created by a group of creative and talented programmers such as Jeff Sutherland and Ken Schwaber. These two people contributed to release of the famous Scrum methodology.

Other advocators of the Agile Manifesto include Ron Jefferies, Kent Beck, and Ward Cunningham. They came up with Extreme Programming methodology. Simply shortened as XP, Extreme Programming was created for programmers that work face-to-face with their customers.

It has many principles and some of them include planning game, small releases with high-value elements, metaphor, simplicity, refactoring, pair programming, testing and sustainable development.

XP methodology emphasizes on customer involvement as well. Customers are called upon to review the features and capabilities of the software product while the development work continues.

Crystal methodology is also featured in the Agile Manifesto. Crystal was created by Alistair Cockburn and it refers to a collection of techniques that Alistair created in order to eliminate an anomaly called software engineering. The foundation of Crystal agile development practices is effective communication and larger teams. Although there are other methodologies, the above is very popular among developers.

To make sure that proper practices are followed when developing software, one should begin by choosing the right programmer.

This is a programmer who is very familiar with agile projects and can provide proof of prior experience.

CHAPTER 10

AGILE SOFTWARE METHODOLOGY

Agile was first introduced in February 2001 via the Agile Manifesto, a document created by a group of developers who met in Snowbird, Utah to discuss the principles behind a way to do lightweight software development.

Since then, the Agile Methodology has grown and been widely adopted by software development teams and companies worldwide.

When we discuss Agile Methodologies, we must also mention Scrum, Lean Software Development, Kanban, Dynamic Systems Development Method (DSDM), and Extreme Programming, since these methodologies all share the same philosophy.

In a nutshell, Agile is about communication, teamwork, collaboration, adaptability, iteration, feedback, and of course, agility! The development initiative is broken down into efforts of short duration and change is not only expected, it is embraced by all stakeholders.

To successfully implement Agile, an organization must embrace its concepts and philosophies at all levels.

Agile provides a framework with which teams can maintain focus on rapidly delivering working software and providing true business value, even in environments where the technical and functional assets and landscape may vary or change routinely.

We can say that Agile allows development teams to provide maximum business value through the delivery of truly valuable, working software that meets the business needs.

How do we know that the software truly meets the business needs? Because all of the stakeholders are involved and quality and scope verification take place, in short, iterative cycles.

Deviations from the true purpose of a feature or piece of functionality can be identified quickly and corrected in an agile manner.

If we go back to the Agile Manifesto, there are 4 key points that it outlines. It favors:

- Individuals and interactions over processes and tools

- Working software over comprehensive documentation

- Customer collaboration over contract negotiation

- Responding to change over following a plan

The key principles behind these points are outlined below:

- Satisfy the customer through early and continuous delivery of working software

- Change is welcomed, even late in the development process

- Working software is delivered frequently, typically at intervals from two weeks to two months

- Developers work directly with functional personnel/SMEs on a daily basis

- Projects are built around motivated, capable people and they are given an environment that allows them to succeed

- Face-to-face communication is critical

- The primary measure of progress is working software

- The development pace must be sustainable

- Continuous attention to technical excellence and good design enhance agility

- Simplicity is essential

- The best architectures and designs emerge from effective, self-organizing teams

- The team routinely reflects on past performance and seeks ways to do things better

If Agile is properly implemented, with buy-in from stakeholders at all levels of the organization, productivity and competitive advantage are maximized and the cost is minimized.

Of course Agile is not necessarily about reducing cost, but when properly implemented and managed that is a side effect that is very nice.

LET'S DISCUSS THE KEY POINTS ABOVE IN GREATER DETAIL.

1.   Favor Individuals and Interactions over Processes and Tools

The greatest processes and tools in the world are worthless without the right people effectively communicating and interacting. Regardless of the size or maturity of the organization, we should start with people then decide the appropriate processes and tools to make our Agile development more effective.

2.   Favor Working Software over Comprehensive Documentation

In the days of waterfall development, With Agile, any documentation that is created is usually created while development takes place. The rapid develop/release approach facilitates concurrency among developers, business analysts, and writers, and in an Agile environment, the business analysts often produce the documentation.

Regardless of the use of Agile or not, it is rare that a customer does not require some type of documentation and there is nothing wrong with that. But, in an organization that is truly Agile-oriented, working software is always the primary, core deliverable.

3.   Favor Customer Collaboration over Contract Negotiation

Let's face it, as long as development teams provide services for customers, there will always be contractual obligations. But when we use the term "contract negotiation" we imply us versus them mentality and this is detrimental to the Agile process!

For the Agile process to be effective, we need contractual vehicles that are flexible and that are developed and written to effectively handle change.

It is not uncommon to work with a client via a Firm Fixed Price (FFP) contract. From the customer's perspective, FFP is preferable because it transfers risk to the service provider.

In this case, Agile is still a valid development methodology, If the customer understands and truly embraces Agile concepts. The difficulty sometimes comes into play when the customer insists on defining functionality up front, forces the service provider to sign a contract whose estimates are based on these initial requirements, then tries to introduce scope creep as the project progresses.

Obviously, an FFP contract is not the preferred vehicle under which to execute Agile, but it is still attainable if all stakeholders are well-versed in and embrace Agile concepts.

4.   Favor Responding to Change over Following a Plan

Although detailed project plans and fancy Gantt charts are impressive, they are not useful with Agile. You read that right! Agile is based on release schedules where the prescribed functionality may be defined, but it is understood that it may change.

Project progress within Agile is based on burndowns. Regardless of the actual functionality delivered, progress is still made over time. The total estimate may change due to newly-identified requirements or scope changes from the customer.

5.   Agile and Risk Management

Prior to the emergence of Agile, a large number of software development projects failed or were canceled with little or no working functionality in place. Teams often spent months or years working on a project with nothing tangible to show for their efforts.

In many cases, projects were developed and delivered only to find that they did not meet the true needs of the business! Imagine after months or years of work and possibly millions of dollars of investment to discover that your needs haven't even been met!

From the project management institute's (PMI) standpoint, risk management is a key knowledge area and something that is very high on the Project Manager's priority list.

All project managers should understand risk. It is just an inherent dynamic within any project and one that has to be understood, and either avoided or mitigated. So, what is a risk? By its formal definition, the risk is something that can or may occur and that could cause unexpected or unanticipated outcomes.

Project managers know that risk is not always something negative. Opportunities are risks as well. But the risk is something that, positive or negative, has to be identified, quantified, and managed. The situation, environment, project, people, etc determine when, where, and how risks are managed.

Agile reduces risk through stakeholder involvement and rapid, iterative development and release. This means that evaluation of scope verification takes place routinely, which effectively reduces risk.

6.   Organizational Threats to Agile

The greatest single threat to Agile is management! More specifically, functional management with unrealistic expectations. In some organizations, Agile is nothing more than a buzzword because the stakeholders have not been educated in its fundamental concepts.

As mentioned earlier, the need for Agile to be understood and embraced by every stakeholder, from the top down.

Without this understanding and support, it will likely fail or at the very least leave managers with a bad taste due to the fact that the development Project Manager tells them "we can certainly modify our approach and give you functionality X but requirement W is going to have to be pushed back to a future iteration."

In the case of FFP, requirement W may just have to drop off entirely!

With Agile, change is welcomed, even late in the development process, but in the case of FFP, it is possible that certain changes can significantly affect the project end date and thus necessitate contract extension.

So, Agile is a software development methodology that fosters rapid delivery of valuable, working software in an iterative manner. It values people and communication over processes and tools. It prefers working software over comprehensive documentation.

It favors active and dynamic involvement of the customer and proper, effective identification of the true needs of the business over contract negotiation. It advocates the ability to nimbly respond to change, even late in the development process to following a detailed, pre-defined plan.

It can be argued whether or not it negates the need to perform risk management, but it is safe to say that with constant and active involvement of the customer and self-organizing, professional, competent, and productive development teams with a true dedication to the customer's mission and a clear understanding of the customer's needs, it can be enormously successful and a win-win for both the customer and the development team.

CHAPTER 11

AGILE BASIC STRATEGY

What's the best way of creating a relevant, high-quality software product? Some say it's agile development. What's so good about it? Saving money is not the forte of agile development (although there are ways to do it).

The main thing is the flexibility of the process and of the product itself - vital relevance for the market.

A quick glance at the main values of the agile approach will allow you to understand whether it suits you and your own business approach:

- Individuals and interactions provide the self-organization and sharing of ideas and experience for the sake of the product quality.

- Working software is more important than comprehensive documentation, which rather distinguishes the waterfall model. You don't deploy documentation - you deploy the product. Your users don't need documentation - they need a great product to use.

  On the other hand, we'd never underestimate the importance of every piece of documentation you have. Although the working result is of higher priority, you should invest into documentation to get the working software faster and with fewer problems on the way.

- Customer collaboration is required to keep the requirements relevant and clarify them in the process of development. You need to communicate with your software company to know that they are building exactly what you want - meanwhile, they are sure they are building the product the way you want. Fruitful collaboration is valued over negotiating contract details - a must for result-oriented teams.

- Responding to change means everything in the mobile world. Your product doesn't run the risks to become dated or incompatible with your business or the mobile environment.

Most software companies embrace agile development, and they apply certain frameworks and methodologies to making your product. Here are five popular ways to Put agile into action.

1.   Scrum

Scrum is a widely used framework to manage projects incrementally: the whole project cycle is divided into short periods of time (sprints), at the end of each the Product Owner receives a tangible part of the software.

One sprint usually lasts 2 weeks. Goals for each subsequent sprint are based on the results achieved at the previous one, they are discussed and approved by the product owner.

Whatever is the amount of work, Scrum allows to divide and manage it efficiently, putting the common output of the team to the forefront. Other priorities are communication, transparency of actions, self-organization, and motivation.

It also values considering technological and business conditions to push the project in the right direction, keeping the work process structured but avoiding excessive bureaucracy.

Put all this together, and you'll get the flexibility to make and maintain a relevant product (satisfaction of the product owner's demands), effective planning of the budget (due to iterational approach), and convenience for the development team, where each voice is valued.

2.   Kanban

Kanban is a technique that prioritizes 'just-in-time' delivery of the software product, inspired by Toyota production system. Although creating software is by no means a mass-production-like making cars, there are certain mechanisms that can be applied in both processes. It's an assembly line where feature requests enter and an improved piece of software comes at the end.

The bottleneck of this line is the limitation. If developers are able to build 4 features over a period of time, and QA can test not more than 3 over the same period, then 3 is the maximum.

Nevertheless, it's easy to define where the bottleneck is (by limiting work-in-progress), and cover the limitations by hiring or redeploying human resources - thus you get efficiency. Visualization of the workflow (as a card wall with cards and columns) allows to manage changes and implement them as planned.

3.   Extreme Programming (XP)

XP is a methodology of software development, intending to boost the quality of software and responsiveness to inevitable changes. It involves short and frequent iterations with unit testing of all code, pair programming (continuous reviewing of the code).

Nothing is coded until it's needed. The common drawback of this approach is the instability of requirements and lack of overall documentation.

The five core values of extreme programming relate to agile in general: communication, simplicity, feedback, courage, and respect. Communication can include the documentation required from the beginning. Simplicity in coding makes it understandable to any other developer; all extra features can be left for later.

Feedback is appreciated from both the team and the end users. Courage must be high enough to rid of the obsolete, irrelevant code, whatever the effort to create it was. Respect applies to the experience and ideas of everyone in the team.

4.   Dynamic Systems Development Method (DSDM)

The main principles behind DSDM are: focus on the business need (delivering the business benefit early); continuous involvement of users; keeping quality at a high level as a must; transparent and proactive control; and building the product iteratively with continuous communication; and timely delivery - the whole scope of work is divided into musts, shoulds, colds, and won't haves in order to meet the deadlines.

5.   Feature-Driven Development (FDD)

Feature-driven development is yet another incremental process, which involves FIVE (5) basic activities: developing the overall model, building a list of features, then planning, designing, and implementing by feature.

The approach unites a set of industry-recognized best practices of software engineering - and the whole became a praised method to timely develop and deliver working software to its owner.

Agile approaches work for software like nothing else and cover the majority of troubles on the way. All else depends on the agile software company you choose, and your own efforts - you need to work closely for the best result. Pay attention to project managers who wield the mastery of agile.

CONCLUSION

Imagine an enterprise software development project where the customer says "we are going to take a long time to get this done and we don't expect to see any results for at least two years".

Can you imagine it? The truth is that it will probably never happen:) So what is a reality? In the real world of enterprise software development, the key for any development team is to provide maximum value to and work closely with the customer, to be able to build a culture of true ingenuity, and to be able to meet the customer's changing needs in a way that there is minimal disruption, if any.

In the early days of software development, it was not uncommon for months to pass before any development began, and once development started, it could be months or years before any type of finished product was ready for testing.

The requirements definition and gathering process was often very long, and in many cases, the development team was isolated from the customer.

Once requirements were complete and development had begun, the change was just not something that was easily entertained.

Let's keep in mind that concepts such as Continuous Integration and Configuration Management were unknown and use of source control repositories was not as mainstream as it is now. A change in requirements was just quite difficult to accommodate and was generally frowned upon.

Constant revision of deadlines and expectations is key to the Agile process. Rather than the traditional (or "old school") methods of managing a project, where what was done could not be undone, as it was discovered too late in the project, Agile takes a constant look at the scope and obstacles a software implementation has and bends to accommodate it in a reasonable manner.

Planning, testing, and integration throughout the project are necessary for a project's success.

Rather than the old-school method where the project manager took the helm, ran the meetings and barked out orders, Agile allows teams to collaborate. Decisions are made as a group to ensure transparency and open communication.

Agile has been slow to be implemented in software system development worldwide, although certain components have been utilized for some time. As more businesses see money and time wasted in using a more rigid project management approach, more are turning to Agile methodologies and practices as a way to stay current, circumvent pitfalls and keep projects on time and under budget. It's your turn now!

www.ingramcontent.com/pod-product-compliance
Lightning Source LLC
Chambersburg PA
CBHW070855070326
40690CB00009B/1853